Bible Puzzler #2

based on stories from Mark's Gospel

CSS Publishing Company, Inc., Lima, Ohio

BIBLE PUZZLER #2

Reprinted in 2002

Copyright © 1985 by
CSS Publishing Company, Inc.
Lima, Ohio

The original purchaser may photocopy material in this publication for use as it was intended (i.e., worship material for worship use; educational material for classroom use; dramatic material for staging or production). No additional permission is required from the publisher for such copying by the original purchaser only. Inquiries should be addressed to: Permissions, CSS Publishing Company, Inc., P.O. Box 4503, Lima, Ohio 45802-4503.

For more information about CSS Publishing Company resources, visit our website at www.csspub.com or e-mail us at custserv@csspub.com or call (800) 241-4056.

ISBN: 978-0-89536-768-6

PRINTED IN U.S.A.

This Puzzle Book Belongs To

Who Received It From

Get the

Mark 1:1-8

The Good News about Jesus was spoken by a man named John. He started preaching in the desert. John's sermon was always the same. He told the people to turn away from their sins and be baptized, then God would forgive them. John looked like a prophet. He wore clothes made of camel's hair, with a leather belt around his waist. Locusts and wild honey were all he ate. Because John baptized people in the River Jordan, he became known as John the Baptizer. It was John's job to get the road ready for the coming of the Lord. That's why we read about John the Baptizer during these weeks before Christmas.

PUZZLE TIME. Most of the answers to this puzzle can be found in today's story. Try to solve it.

Across
1. Today's story is about a man who was called the _ _ _ _ _ _ _ _.
2. The name of the man in today's story is _ _ _ _.
3. This was the place where the preaching about Jesus began. _ _ _ _ _ _
4. _ _ _ _ _ _ _ and wild honey were John's favorite foods.
5. John was _ _ _ _ by God to prepare the way of the Lord.
6. Many _ _ _ and women were baptized by John.

Down
1. John wore a leather _ _ _ _ around his waist.
2. _ _ _ _ _ was John's cousin.
7. John was a _ _ _ who was given a special job by the Lord.
8. John _ _ _ strange foods and dressed in unusual clothes.
9. John _ _ _ _ an outfit made of camel's hair.
10. John told the people to give up _ _ _ of their sins.
11. To _ _ _ _ away from sin means to repent.

Road Ready

WORD SCRAMBLE. These words from today's story got all mixed up. Try to straighten them out; then write them in the space provided.

1. OHJN
2. DANRJO
3. ORLD
4. ODG

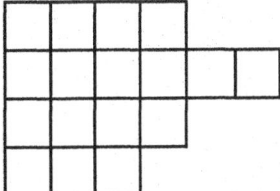

Living With

Mark 1:9-15

When John baptized Jesus in the Jordan River, the Spirit came down like a dove. A voice from heaven said, "You are my own dear Son. I am well pleased with you." Right after this happened, the Spirit made Jesus go into

HIDDEN MESSAGE. There is a message hiding in the words and letters below. Just follow the number one until you form a word. Do the same for each number until you have the entire message. Write it in the space below.

9	2	8	1	9	3	6	2	8	2	7	2
P	S	T	T	R	S	T	P	O	I	D	R

7	4	6	1	3	4	9	3	4	5	2	6	4
E	J	H	H	E	E	A	N	S	I	I	E	U

3	5	4	1	5	2	7	7	5	7	9	7
T	N	S	E	T	T	S	E	O	R	Y	T

Write the message here: _____

_____

Wild Animals

the desert. Jesus stayed there for forty days. The devil came and tempted him, and wild beasts visited him, too. But Jesus was all right because angels came and helped him.

HIDDEN WORDS. These words from today's story are hiding in the letters below. They might be going up or down, forward or backward, or even diagonally. Circle the ones you find.

Words							
John	J	O	H	N	F	A	H	D
Devil								
Jordan	O	A	B	S	O	N	E	O
Wild								
River	R	I	V	E	R	G	A	V
Beasts	D	L	I	W	T	E	V	E
Forty								
Angels	A	A	C	D	Y	L	E	D
Dove								
Son	N	E	Y	G	H	S	N	E
Voice	F	D	E	S	E	R	T	V
Heaven								
Desert	E	C	I	O	V	I	J	I
Days	B	E	A	S	T	S	X	L

Fishing

Mark 1:14-20

The Gospel of Mark tells this story about Jesus calling his first disciples. One day Jesus went walking along the shore of Lake Galilee. There he saw two fishermen, Simon and his brother Andrew. They were catching fish with their net. Jesus said to them, "Come with me. I will teach you to catch

HIDDEN MESSAGE. There is a message hiding in the numbers and letters below. Just follow the number one until you form a word. Do the same for each of the other numbers until you have the entire message, then write it in the space below.

2	4	8	1	6	3	2	4	1	4	5	2
P	T	C	J	D	T	R	E	E	A	T	O

6	8	1	6	4	6	1	6	5	9	2
I	A	S	S	C	C	U	I	H	P	M

4	6	2	1	2	3	6	2	6	5	2
H	P	I	S	S	O	L	E	E	E	D

9	6	8	7	9	8	9	7	9	8	9
E	S	T	T	O	C	P	O	L	H	E

Write the message here: _____

_____

for People

people!" Simon and Andrew left their nets and followed Jesus. As they walked along, they saw two other brothers, James and John. They were getting their nets ready in their boat. When Jesus called them, they stopped what they were doing and went with him.

HIDDEN WORDS. These words from today's story are hiding in the letters below. Some of them are going up or down, some are going forward or backward, and some even appear diagonally. Circle the ones you find.

Gospel
John
Fish
Mark
Simon
Lake
Boat
Net
First
Story
Catch
Shore
Went

G	O	S	P	E	L	F	M	S
W	E	R	D	N	A	I	A	I
N	E	T	C	H	K	S	R	M
A	B	N	A	O	E	H	K	O
B	O	A	T	J	C	D	E	N
E	M	O	C	F	I	R	S	T
E	R	O	H	S	T	O	R	Y

Wrestling

Mark 1:21-28

Jesus went to the Jewish place of worship — the synagogue — so that he could teach the people. They were all amazed at how much he knew. One day he even healed a man who came into the synagogue. This man had an evil spirit which screamed at Jesus, "What do you want with us, Jesus of Nazareth? Are you here to get rid of us? You are God's holy messenger!" When Jesus ordered the spirit to be quiet and to leave the man, it did! Everyone was amazed! The news about Jesus began to spread everywhere.

MIX AND MATCH. Match the word in the second column with the right number in the first column. Look at today's story for some help.

1. Jewish place of worship _____ a. Devil
2. God's holy messenger _____ b. Nazareth
3. Hometown of Jesus _____ c. Jesus
4. Another name for evil spirit _____ d. Synagogue

With Evil

PUZZLE TIME. You can find most of the answers to this puzzle in today's story.

Across
1. Jesus often went to the Jewish place of _ _ _ _ _ _ _, the synagogue.
2. A man who had an _ _ _ _ spirit screamed at Jesus.
3. Jesus went to the synagogue to _ _ _ _ _ the people.
4. The spirit asked Jesus, "What do you _ _ _ _ with us?"
5. First you have to sow the seed; then you can _ _ _ _ the harvest.

Down
6. The demon thought Jesus was God's _ _ _ _ messenger.
7. The demon asked Jesus if he was there to get _ _ _ of the evil spirits.
8. The _ _ _ _ _ _ were amazed at this miracle which Jesus performed.
9. The _ _ _ _ _ _ in the man was an evil one.
10. The people were surprised at _ _ _ much Jesus knew.

Jesus Makes

Mark 1:29-39

One day Jesus and his disciples went to the home of Simon and Andrew. Simon's mother-in-law was sick in bed with a fever. Jesus went to her, took her by the hand, and helped her get up. All of a sudden, the fever left her! So she started to cook a meal for the guests. When evening came, the people

HIDDEN MESSAGE. There is a message hiding in the numbers and letters below. Just follow the number one until you form a word. Do the same for all the rest of the numbers. When you find the whole message, write it in the space below.

2	7	3	1	7	2	6	5	1	7	1	5
M	W	I	S	I	O	S	W	I	T	M	A
8	2	7	6	2	9	2	4	9	2	1	
A	T	H	I	H	F	E	L	E	R	O	
9	4	1	1	6	5	9	6	3	9	4	
V	A	N	S	C	S	E	K	N	R	W	

Write the message here: _____

_____

Us Well

of the town began to bring those who were sick to Jesus, and he healed many of them. Very early the next morning, Jesus went out of town to find a quiet place to pray. But his disciples found him. They said, "Everyone is looking for you!" Jesus said that he had to go to other villages, too, so that he could teach the people and heal the sick.

HIDDEN WORDS. These words from today's story are hiding in the letters below. They might be going up or down, forward or backward, or even diagonally. Circle the ones you find.

Jesus
Cook
Home
Meal
Simon
Town
Sick
Healed
Bed
Place
Fever
Teach
Hand
Pray
Helped

```
H  O  M  E  L  A  E  M  A
B  D  S  I  M  O  N  R  D
J  E  S  U  S  P  W  E  E
Y  P  D  C  I  L  O  V  L
A  L  N  O  C  A  T  E  A
R  E  A  O  K  C  A  F  E
P  H  H  K  T  E  A  C  H
```

Teaching With

Mark 4:26-34

When Jesus preached to the people, he used parables, or stories, to help them understand what he was saying. One day Jesus said that the Kingdom of God was like a man who scatters seed in his field. The man goes about his usual work each day and all the while those seeds are growing and sprouting. Before long the man's field is full of wheat, so he cuts it down

HIDDEN WORDS. These words from today's story are hiding in the letters below. They might be going up or down, forward or backward, or even diagonally. Circle the ones you find.

Jesus
Work
Birds
Parables
Day
Full
Stories
Wheat
God
Good
Man
Soil
Seed
Grows
Field
Nests

```
J  E  S  U  S  A  S  B  C
G  H  E  N  A  M  T  E  D
O  O  E  J  L  I  O  S  F
O  I  D  A  Y  G  R  N  S
D  L  E  I  F  K  I  E  W
P  A  R  A  B  L  E  S  O
W  H  E  A  T  L  S  T  R
B  I  R  D  S  M  N  S  G
W  O  R  K  F  U  L  L  O
```

Pictures

with his sickle. The good soil helped all of those seeds grow into fine stalks of wheat.

Jesus also said that the Kingdom of God was like a little mustard seed. The mustard seed starts out as the tiniest seed of all, but it soon grows into one of the largest plants. Even the birds could make their nests in its branches. What was Jesus trying to say about the Kingdom of God?

HIDDEN MESSAGE. There is a message hiding in the words and numbers below. Just follow the number one until you form a word. Do the same for all of the other numbers. Then write the entire message in the space below.

2	8	5	1	3	2	3	6	2	9
K	T	I	T	O	I	F	L	N	S
4	1	8	1	6	2	4	5	9	2
G	H	I	E	I	G	O	S	E	D
4	8	6	2	7	9	6	2	9	8
D	N	K	O	A	E	E	M	D	Y

Write the message here: _____

_____

Stormy

Mark 4:35-41

One night Jesus and his disciples decided to take their boat to the other side of the lake. All of a sudden a very strong wind blew up and the boat began to fill up with water. The disciples were very frightened so they called to Jesus — who was asleep — and said, "Don't you care that we are about to

WORD SCRAMBLE. These words from today's story got all mixed up. Try to straighten them out.

1. ESUSJ
2. TERWA
3. OATB
4. ERAC
5. EROM

Water

die?" So Jesus got up and said to the wind, "Be quiet!" Then he said to the waves, "Be still!" The wind and the waves did what Jesus told them to do! This made the disciples even more afraid than they were before.

HIDDEN WORDS. These words from today's story are hiding in the letters below. They might be going up or down, forward or backward, or even diagonally. Circle the ones you find.

Night
Asleep
Boat
Jesus
Lake
Die
Strong
Still
Wind
Waves
Water
Disciples
Blew
Afraid
Care

N	I	G	H	T	C	D	W	A
D	I	S	C	I	P	L	E	S
I	I	T	A	O	B	S	L	L
A	L	E	W	S	J	T	B	E
R	A	W	A	T	E	R	E	E
F	K	I	V	I	S	O	R	P
A	E	N	E	L	U	N	A	E
A	B	D	S	L	S	G	C	F

The Girl Who

Mark 5:21-43

A man named Jairus came to Jesus one day with a sad story. His little girl was sick and about to die. Jairus knelt at Jesus' feet and begged him to heal her. As Jesus was walking to Jairus' house, many people followed him and crowded around him. One woman, who had been sick for many years, just

PUZZLE TIME. The answers to this puzzle can be found in today's story. Try to solve it.

Across
1. The man who came to see Jesus was named _ _ _ _ _ _.
2. When Jesus came to the little girl's house, everyone was very _ _ _.
3. This _ _ _ _ _ is about a little girl who died and was made well by Jesus.
4. A sick woman touched Jesus' _ _ _ _ _ _ _ when he was walking to the little girl's house.
5. The sick woman was _ _ _ _ _ _ of her illness just by touching Jesus!

Down
1. _ _ _ _ _ asked all of the neighbors to leave the little girl's house.
6. After Jesus made her well, the little girl got up and began to _ _ _ _ _.
7. Jesus told the girl's parents to give her something to _ _ _.
8. Everyone was crying because the little girl had _ _ _ _.
9. This story is about two miracles which happened to two people — a very sick _ _ _ _ _ and a little girl.
10. Jesus took the little girl by the _ _ _ _ and told her to get up.
11. The woman who touched Jesus had been _ _ _ _ for many years.

Died Too Soon

touched his clothes so that she would be healed — she was! Before Jesus could get to Jairus' house, the little girl died. So Jesus went into the house, got rid of all the neighbors who were standing around weeping and wailing, and went into the little girl's bedroom. He took her hand and said, "Little girl! Get up, I tell you!" The little girl got up and started to dance around! Jesus told her parents to give her something to eat.

The Home

Mark 6:1-6

Jesus decided to go back to his home town of Nazareth to preach to the people and teach in their synagogues. But he was very surprised when he got there because no one believed in him. They said, "How did he get so smart? Isn't he a carpenter, the son of Mary and Joseph? How can someone

HIDDEN MESSAGE. There is a message hiding in the numbers and letters below. Just follow the number one until you find a word. Do the same for the other numbers. When you have the entire message, write it in the space below.

2	8	4	1	6	5	3	6	1	8	4	9
W	H	A	J	H	I	N	I	E	O	C	T

7	2	3	4	9	4	1	8	4	4	1	7
O	A	O	C	O	E	S	M	P	T	U	W

2	9	4	5	8	6	9	4	1	7	3
S	W	E	N	E	S	N	D	S	N	T

Write the message here: _____

Town Boy

like him perform miracles?" Jesus said to the people, "A prophet is accepted everywhere except in his own hometown." So he couldn't perform any miracles there because the people didn't have any faith.

HIDDEN WORDS. These words from today's story are hiding in the letters below. They might be going up or down, forward or backward, or even diagonally. Circle the ones you find.

Preach
Prophet
Home
Joseph
Teach
People
No
Town
Smart
Miracles
Son
Faith
Mary
Back
His

S	I	H	M	A	R	Y	T	B
M	O	P	E	O	P	L	E	A
A	O	N	E	M	O	H	A	C
R	P	R	E	A	C	H	C	K
T	E	H	P	O	R	P	H	A
M	I	R	A	C	L	E	S	B
J	O	S	E	P	H	E	D	C
N	W	O	T	F	A	I	T	H

Jesus'

Mark 6:7-13

One day Jesus called the twelve disciples together and told them that they were going to go out on a preaching mission! He was going to send them out two by two, and he gave them power to heal and to drive out evil spirits. They were not to take anything with them at all — no food, no money, no

PUZZLE TIME. The answers to this puzzle can be found in today's lesson. Try to solve it.

Across
1. Today's lesson is about the disciples' first _ _ _ _ _ _ _ _ _ _ journey.
2. Jesus told the disciples to leave the towns that wouldn't _ _ _ _ _ _ to them.
3. The disciples were supposed to _ _ _ _ _ the dust from their feet when they left an unfriendly town.
4. Jesus decided to _ _ _ _ the disciples out two by two.
5. Jesus gave the disciples the power to _ _ _ _ the sick.

Down
1. The disciples were not allowed to take any _ _ _ _ _ with them on their journey.
4. The disciples received power to drive out evil _ _ _ _ _ _ _.
6. The disciples _ _ _ _ _ _ _ _ _ to the people about turning away from sin.
7. Those who were Jesus' special followers were called _ _ _ _ _ _ _ _ _.

Preachers

extra clothes. Jesus told them to stay wherever people were friendly to them but to leave those towns where the people would not listen to them. They were supposed to shake the dust from their feet after leaving an unfriendly town! So the disciples went off on their first missionary journey and preached to the people about turning away from their sins.

The World's

Mark 6:30-34

Jesus and his disciples were always busy because people kept coming to see Jesus. Sometimes they didn't even have time to eat. One day Jesus and the disciples decided to get into their boat and go somewhere where they could be alone and rest. But the people figured out where they were going and got to the place before Jesus did. When Jesus saw all the people, he felt

HIDDEN MESSAGE. There is a message hiding in the numbers and letters below. Just follow the number one until you fine a word. Do the same for the other numbers then write the whole message in the space below.

2	7	8	3	5	6	4	1	7	4	5	9
A	G	B	H	H	A	F	J	R	R	A	P
2	9	4	1	9	3	7	4	7	2	9	4
N	I	I	E	C	I	E	E	A	D	N	N
5	1	7	3	4	1	9	8	9	4	8	1
D	S	T	S	D	U	I	I	C	S	G	S

Write the message here: _____

_____

Largest Lunch

sorry for them, so he taught them about many things. When it was getting late, the disciples told Jesus to send the people home; but Jesus decided to have a little picnic instead. The disciples could only find five loaves of bread and two fish but that turned out to be enough. Jesus blessed it and passed the food out to the people. Everyone had plenty to eat and there was even some left over! It was a wonderful picnic.

WORD SCRAMBLE. These words from today's story got all mixed up. Try to straighten them out, then write them in the space provided.

1. EOPLPE
2. SHFI
3. ECLAP
4. ENOLA
5. IFEV
6. ISCDIPLES

Rules That

Mark 7:1-8, 14-15, 21-23

Jesus and his disciples often got into trouble with the leaders of the Jewish people. Usually it was because they didn't follow some of the rules of the Jewish religion. One of these rules had to do with eating. Jewish people were supposed to wash their hands a certain way before they ate. One day

FILL IN THE BLANKS. Choose the correct word, taken from today's lesson, to complete the following sentences.

Trouble	Praying	Hypocrites
Hearts	Eating	Sneaky

1. Jesus and his disciples sometimes got into _____ with the Jewish leaders.
2. One of the Jewish rules had to do with _____.
3. Jesus called the religious leaders _____.
4. Jesus said that these religious leaders didn't worship God with their _____.

Don't Work

the Jewish leaders asked Jesus why his disciples didn't follow the rules about washing their hands. Jesus told the Jewish leaders exactly what he thought of them. He called them "hypocrites" which means that they said one thing but did another. They didn't honor and worship God with their hearts!

HIDDEN WORDS. These words from today's story are hiding in the letters below. They might be going up or down, forward or backward, or even diagonally. Circle the ones you find.

Disciples								
Trouble	D	I	S	C	I	P	L	E	S
Jewish	O	A	B	C	H	O	N	O	R
Rules								
Eating	G	N	I	T	A	E	D	E	U
Wash	A	D	A	Y	N	H	F	G	L
Hands								
Ate	A	T	O	L	D	S	I	J	E
Day								
Told	K	L	E	M	S	A	I	D	S
Said	N	O	H	S	I	W	E	J	P
Honor								
God	H	E	A	R	T	S	Q	R	S
Hearts	T	E	L	B	U	O	R	T	U

open

Mark 7:31-37

Once there was a man who could not hear and who could hardly talk. His friends felt so sorry for him that they decided to try and help him. So they took him to Jesus and begged him to heal the man. Jesus took the man away from all the people. Then he touched the man's ears and anointed the man's tongue with saliva. Jesus looked up to heaven and said, "Open up!" All of a sudden, the man was able to hear and to talk! He was very happy and so were his friends. They wanted to tell everyone about this great miracle, but Jesus told them to keep it a secret. It was such a wonderful thing that the people just had to share this good news. Pretty soon everyone was talking about Jesus and how he could make the deaf to hear and the dumb to talk again.

WORD SCRAMBLE. These words from today's lesson got all mixed up. Try to straighten them out then write them in the space provided.

1. EARH
2. ARE
3. LKTA
4. LLET

Up!

PUZZLE TIME. The answers to this puzzle can be found in today's story. Try to solve it.

Across
1. This word means that you cannot hear. _ _ _ _
2. Jesus performed a wonderful _ _ _ _ _ _ _ for the man in today's story.
3. Jesus _ _ _ _ the people to keep this wonderful healing a secret.
4. The man in today's story could not hear or _ _ _ _.
5. Jesus looked up to heaven and _ _ _ _ something very powerful.
6. Jesus told the man's mouth and ears to "_ _ _ _ up!"
7. "Good _ _ _ _" is another way of saying "Gospel."

Down
8. We could use this word to describe this miracle. _ _ _ _ _ _ _ _ _
9. Jesus _ _ _ _ _ _ _ _ the man's tongue with saliva.
10. The deaf man's _ _ _ _ _ _ _ really wanted to help him.

Who Do You

Mark 8:27-38

One day Jesus and his disciples were taking a trip from one town to another. Since they were walking, they had a lot of time to talk. So Jesus asked them a question: "Tell me, who do people say that I am?" The disciples answered, "Some people think that you are John the Baptizer. Others think that you are the prophet Elijah or one of the other prophets." Then

HIDDEN MESSAGE. There is a message hiding for you in the numbers and letters below. Just follow the number one until you find a word. Do the same for each of the other numbers, then write the message in the space below.

2	9	8	1	9	4	7	2	5	2
G	Q	J	P	U	V	T	A	G	V

9	6	9	4	5	1	6	3	9	2
E	A	S	E	O	E	N	A	T	E

7	8	5	6	1	8	6	4	9	8
O	E	O	S	T	S	W	R	I	U

9	1	6	4	9	8	1	5	6
O	E	E	Y	N	S	R	D	R

Write the message here: _____

_____

Say I Am?

Jesus asked them, "But who do you say I am?" Peter had the answer. "You are the Messiah." There was another time when Peter didn't make Jesus quite so happy. Jesus told the disciples that he would be put to death, but three days later would rise to life. Peter didn't like this at all, and he told Jesus what he thought. Peter's words made Jesus angry. Jesus said that he had to do God's work and that meant giving up his life.

HIDDEN WORDS. These words from today's story are hiding in the letters below. Some of them are going up and down, some are going forward and backward, and some are even going diagonally. Circle the ones you find.

Jesus
Answer
Town
Three
Question
Life
Peter
Talk
Death
John
Rise
Days
Trip
Time
Who

J	E	S	U	S	R	E	T	E	P
T	O	W	N	Y	E	A	B	K	R
R	W	H	O	A	M	E	L	F	I
I	C	D	N	D	I	A	G	H	S
P	Q	U	E	S	T	I	O	N	E
R	E	W	S	N	A	E	F	I	L
T	H	R	E	E	H	T	A	E	D

Carrying

Mark 8:31-38

One day Jesus began to tell his disciples about all of the things that were going to happen to him. He said that he would suffer. The leaders of the Jewish people would turn their backs on him. He would even be put to death! These words of Jesus made the Apostle Peter very upset. Peter took

HIDDEN WORDS. The following words from today's lesson are hiding in the letters below. Some of them are going up or down, some are going forward or backward, and some are even hiding diagonally. Circle the ones you find.

Jesus	J	E	S	U	S	D	E	F	D
Follow									
Tell	G	L	L	E	T	G	H	S	I
Death									
Disciples	F	O	L	L	O	W	I	S	S
Will	W	W	D	E	A	T	H	O	C
Angry									
Words	I	O	A	N	G	R	Y	R	I
Cross									
Peter	L	R	T	U	R	N	J	C	P
God	L	D	C	P	E	T	E	R	L
Apostles									
People	A	S	P	E	O	P	L	E	E
Turn	B	A	P	O	S	T	L	E	S

Our Cross

Jesus aside and told him that those terrible things couldn't ever happen to Jesus. Jesus became angry with Peter, because the apostle was not helping Jesus do God's will. Then Jesus told all the people that they would have to carry a cross, too, if they wanted to follow him.

HIDDEN MESSAGE. There is a message hiding for you in the numbers and letters below. Just follow the number one until you form a word; do the same for all the other numbers, then write the message in the space provided.

2	5	6	1	4	8	2	1	3	1
O	T	C	F	H	C	F	O	J	L

8	4	6	1	5	3	3	6	1	7
R	A	A	L	O	E	S	R	O	T

4	8	3	6	1	4	8	3	8	1
V	O	U	R	W	E	S	S	S	E

9	6	7	1	7	9	1	7	9	7
T	Y	H	R	E	O	S	I	O	R

Write the message here: _____

The Strange

Mark 9:2-9

One day Jesus took Peter, James, and John to a high mountain. While they were there, a very strange thing happened. Jesus' whole body began to glow so brightly that the disciples could hardly look at him. Then another strange thing happened. The disciples saw Moses and Elijah talking to Jesus!

PUZZLE TIME. Most of the answers to this puzzle can be found in today's story. Try to solve it.

Across
1. Jesus took three of the disciples to a high _ _ _ _ _ _ _ _.
2. Jesus' entire _ _ _ _ began to shine.
3. It was very hard for the disciples to _ _ _ _ at Jesus.
4. When the disciples looked up, they didn't _ _ _ anyone but Jesus.
5. Peter, James, and _ _ _ _ went to the mountain with Jesus.
6. This was the Old Testament person who received the Ten Commandments. _ _ _ _ _

Down
2. The body of Jesus began to shine _ _ _ _ _ _ _ _.
5. This disciple went with Peter and John to the high mountain on the day Jesus was transfigured. _ _ _ _ _
7. The voice said, "This is my own dear _ _ _."
8. The building in which we live is called a _ _ _ _ _.
9. A great _ _ _ _ _ came over the disciples while they were on the mountain.
10. Jesus asked the disciples not to _ _ _ _ anyone about what had happened.
11. The voice from the cloud must have belonged to _ _ _.

Change

Peter, James, and John were so frightened that they didn't know what to do or say. A great cloud hovered over them and out of it came a voice which said, "This is my own dear Son — listen to him!" When the disciples looked up again, they didn't see anyone but Jesus. He told them not to tell anyone about what had happened. We call this event the Transfiguration of Jesus.

Who's More

Mark 9:30-37

One day Jesus caught his disciples having a talk about who was the greatest disciple among them. Jesus asked them what they were saying, but they were ashamed to tell him. So Jesus reminded them that whoever wanted to be the greatest would have to be the last, the servant of all the rest. Really

HIDDEN WORDS. These words from today's story are hiding in the letters below. They might be going up or down, forward or backward, or even diagonally. Circle the ones you find.

Jesus
Who
Last
Care
Ones
Love
Child
Talk
Greatest
Tell
Rest
Him
Eyes
Little
Father

J	E	S	U	S	O	M	A	L
L	L	E	T	E	N	I	B	I
O	A	D	E	Y	E	H	C	T
V	F	S	R	E	S	T	E	T
E	F	A	T	H	E	R	R	L
G	D	L	I	H	C	H	A	E
T	A	L	K	W	H	O	C	I
G	R	E	A	T	E	S	T	J

Important?

great people — in the Lord's eyes — are not the ones who try to be great, but those who care about other people. Jesus picked up a little child and told the disciples that they should love children like this and treat them nicely. Then they would be doing what Jesus and his Father wanted them to do.

WORD SCRAMBLE. These words from today's story got all mixed up. Try to straighten them out, then write them in the space provided.

1. REATG
2. REWE
3. ESUSJ
4. REAC
5. OT
6. YEES
7. TASL
8. LATK

G			
R		
E			
A		
T	
E		
S		
T		

Doing Miracles

Mark 9:38-50

The disciples became upset because some people were trying to perform miracles in the name of Jesus. Jesus told them not to worry about it because those people who really believe in him would soon be found out. Those who were against Jesus would also be discovered. Jesus gave a very strong warning about tempting other people and giving a bad example. Anyone who caused someone else to lose his faith in Jesus would be punished. Jesus said that we should get rid of those things that cause us to sin.

HIDDEN MESSAGE. There is a message hiding in the numbers and letters below. Just follow the number one until you find a word. Do the same for all of the other numbers. Then write the message in the space below.

2	8	1	5	3	9	6	5	8	2	3	4	6
W	F	T	J	A	O	W	E	O	H	R	A	I

2	8	1	9	4	5	1	4	6	5	9	4
O	U	H	U	G	S	O	A	L	U	T	I

8	5	1	3	4	7	1	4	6	4	7	8
N	S	S	E	N	B	E	S	L	T	E	D

Write the message here: _____

_____

for Jesus

PUZZLE TIME. The answers to this puzzle can be found in today's story. Try to solve it.

Across
1. The people who were upset in today's story were the _ _ _ _ _ _ _ _ _.
2. Some imposters were doing miracles in the name of _ _ _ _ _.
3. Anyone who causes someone else to lose his _ _ _ _ _ will be punished.
4. Jesus is the _ _ _ of God.

Down
5. Giving a bad example could cause someone to _ _ _ _ her faith.
6. Strangers were performing _ _ _ _ _ _ _ _ in the name of Jesus.
7. Jesus told us to get rid of those things that cause us to _ _ _.

Let the

Mark 10:2-16

Jesus taught the people many things while he was on this earth. One of his lessons was about children. Some people brought their children to Jesus one day so that he could bless them. But the disciples scolded the people. They probably thought that Jesus was too busy or too tired to spend time with children. Jesus became angry with his disciples and said to them: "Let

HIDDEN WORDS. These words from today's story are hiding in the letters below. They might be going up or down, forward or backward, or even diagonally. Circle the ones you find.

Earth
Told
People
Bless
Spend
Stop
Come
Kingdom
God
Lessons
Child
Busy
Enter
Time
Let
Arms

E	A	R	T	H	A	B	B	S
L	B	E	C	D	M	E	U	T
P	L	E	S	S	O	N	S	O
O	E	M	O	C	D	T	Y	P
E	S	M	R	A	G	E	T	E
P	S	D	O	G	N	R	O	M
D	L	I	H	C	I	E	L	I
S	P	E	N	D	K	F	D	T

Children Come

the children come to me. Do not stop them! The Kingdom of God is filled with people like these children." Then Jesus said something even more important. He told them that unless they received the Kingdom of God like a child, they would never be able to enter it. After he taught this lesson, Jesus took the children in his arms and blessed them.

WORD SCRAMBLE. These words from today's story got all mixed up. Try to straighten them out. Then write them in the space provided.

1. OOKT
2. MITE
3. ENO
4. DOG
5. DAIS
6. OT
7. MSRA

How to Find

Mark 10:17-30

One day a young man ran up to Jesus, knelt at his feet and asked him this question: "Good Teacher, what must I do to receive eternal life?" Jesus said that he should keep the commandments. But the man said that he had been doing that ever since he was very young. Jesus looked upon this man with

PUZZLE TIME. The answers to this puzzle can be found in today's story. Try to solve it.

Across
1. This word means "to last forever." _ _ _ _ _ _ _
2. Jesus told the young man to _ _ _ _ his belongings.
3. The young man in today's story must have had a lot of _ _ _ _ _.
4. Jesus was trying to help the young man enter the kingdom of _ _ _.

Down
2. The young man became very _ _ _ when he heard Jesus' words.
3. Today's story is about a young _ _ _ who asked Jesus a question.
5. Eternal _ _ _ _ is another way of talking about heaven.
6. The young man _ _ _ _ _ at Jesus' feet.
7. The young man must have been very _ _ _ _.
8. The young man placed himself at Jesus' _ _ _ _ because that was a sign of respect.

Eternal Life

love and said to him, "You need to do only one more thing. Go and sell everything you have and give the money to the poor and you will have riches in heaven. Then come and follow me." But the young man became very sad because he was very rich. Jesus told his disciples that it was very hard for rich people to enter the Kingdom of God. The disciples wondered how *anyone* could be saved! Jesus said that for people to save themselves was impossible, but for God, everything was possible.

Who Gets the

Mark 10:35-45

Two of the apostles, James and John, came to Jesus one day with a special request. They asked him if they could sit with Jesus in the kingdom — one at his right hand and one at his left. Jesus told them that they didn't know what they were asking. Could they drink the cup of suffering that he would drink? James and John said that they could. Jesus agreed that they would

HIDDEN QUESTION. There is a question hiding for you in the numbers and letters below. Just follow the number one until you find a word. Do the same for all of the other numbers, then write the question in the space provided. Do you know the answer?

2	7	3	1	6	4	2	7	3	1	5	4
T	P	D	N	S	W	H	L	I	A	W	H

7	6	3	8	5	3	6	8	1	9	3	7
A	P	S	I	A	C	E	N	M	H	I	C

5	6	9	1	2	6	3	9	4	7	5
N	C	E	E	E	I	P	A	O	E	T

9	5	3	9	6	3	9	6	3	5	7
V	E	L	E	A	E	N	L	S	D	S

Write the question here: _____

Best Seats?

suffer some day, but he also told them that it wasn't right to decide who would have special places in the kingdom. Only God would make those decisions. Then Jesus reminded all of the disciples again that anyone who wanted to be great had to be the servant of the rest. Even he, Jesus, did not come to earth to receive honor but to serve others and to give up his life.

HIDDEN WORDS. These words from today's story are hiding in the letters below. They might be going up or down, forward or backward, or even diagonally. Circle the ones you find.

Apostles
Right
God
Jesus
Drink
Great
Hand
Special
Earth
Cup
Serve
James
Suffer
Give
Sit
Told
Life
Left
Places

A	P	O	S	T	L	E	S	S
J	U	A	I	B	A	A	C	U
A	C	S	K	N	I	R	D	F
M	G	I	V	E	C	T	N	F
E	V	R	E	S	E	H	A	E
S	U	S	E	J	P	D	H	R
P	L	A	C	E	S	E	F	G
G	O	D	R	I	G	H	T	H
T	F	E	L	T	O	L	D	J
G	R	E	A	T	L	I	F	E

Can You

Mark 10:46-52

One day as Jesus was leaving the town of Jericho, he passed near a blind beggar who was sitting by the road. When this beggar heard that Jesus was near, he started shouting, "Jesus! Son of David! Have mercy on me!" The people scolded him and told him to be quiet, but he kept shouting all the louder, "Son of David, have mercy on me!" Jesus stopped and asked the man to come to him. So the blind man threw off his cloak, jumped up, and went to Jesus. "What do you want me to do for you?" Jesus asked him. The blind man answered, "Teacher, I want to see again." "Go," said Jesus. "Your faith has made you see." The blind man was suddenly able to see. He was so happy that he followed Jesus down the road!

WORD SCRAMBLE. These words from today's story got all mixed up. Try to straighten them out, then write them in the space provided.

1. ANM
2. EES
3. DOAR
4. MEOC
5. PHPAY

Believe It?

PUZZLE TIME. The answers to this puzzle can be found in today's story. Try to solve it.

Across
1. This was the name given to Jesus by the blind man. _ _ _ _ _ _ _
2. Jesus asked the blind man to _ _ _ _ to him.
3. The blind man called Jesus, "_ _ _ of David."
4. Jesus told the blind man that his faith had _ _ _ _ him well.
5. The blind man was sitting by the side of the _ _ _ _.
6. The blind man _ _ _ suddenly able to see.

Down
4. The blind man asked Jesus to have _ _ _ _ _ on him.
7. _ _ _ _ _ was leaving the town of Jericho when he met the blind man.
8. When the blind man _ _ _ _ _ that Jesus was near, he started to shout.
9. The blind man was a poor _ _ _ _ _ _.
10. The man's problem was that he was _ _ _ _ _.

The Best

Mark 12:28b-34

One day a Jewish teacher came to Jesus with a question: "Which commandment is the most important of all?" Jesus answered him right away. The most important one is this: "Love the Lord your God with all your

HIDDEN MESSAGE. There is a message hiding for you in the letters and numbers below. Just follow the number one until you find a word. Do the same for the other numbers. Then write the entire message in the space below.

6	1	7	4	2	5	3	6	1	4	8
F	J	T	I	P	C	T	R	E	M	O

2	7	5	9	6	5	2	6	4	7	5
I	H	O	T	O	M	C	M	P	E	M

9	2	8	3	4	4	2	9	9	1	9
E	K	L	W	O	R	E	S	T	S	A

4	5	4	1	5	2	9	8	5	4	5
T	A	A	U	N	D	M	D	D	N	M

5	5	9	5	9	1	9	5	3	4
E	N	E	T	N	S	S	O	T	T

Write the message here: _____

Commandment

heart, with all your soul, with all your mind, and with all your strength." The second most important commandment, said Jesus, is this one: "Love your neighbor as you love yourself." The teacher of the law was very impressed with Jesus' answer. He congratulated him, saying, "Well done, Teacher!" Jesus told the man that he wasn't far himself from the Kingdom of God, for he was a very wise person.

HIDDEN WORDS. These words from today's story are hiding in the letters below. They might be going up or down, forward or backward, or even diagonally. Circle the ones you find.

Teacher
Right
Away
God
Heart
Mind
Strength
Self
Law
Wise
Jesus
Person
Love
Man
Soul
Neighbor

T	E	A	C	H	E	R	A	P
M	R	I	G	H	T	C	B	E
J	A	E	S	I	W	Y	T	R
E	F	N	D	E	A	A	R	S
S	E	L	F	M	L	W	A	O
U	G	O	D	I	G	A	E	N
S	T	R	E	N	G	T	H	H
E	V	O	L	D	S	O	U	L
N	E	I	G	H	B	O	R	I

When the Time

Mark 13:14-32

Jesus gave us some hints or signs to look for that would tell us when the Son of Man was coming back to earth. There would first be lots of trouble. Terrible things would happen and people would pretend to be the Messiah — but they would be lying. Then the sun would grow dark and the moon

WORD SCRAMBLE. These words from today's story got all mixed up. Try to straighten them out, then write them in the space provided.

1. GNSIS
2. OT
3. NOOM
4. NO
5. LLUF
6. ROMF
7. LLA
8. NDSE

Runs Out

would no longer shine. The stars would fall from heaven and the Son of Man will appear, riding on a cloud, full of power and glory. He will send the angels out to all the corners of the world to gather together God's chosen people!

HIDDEN WORDS. These words from today's story are hiding in the letters below. They might be going up or down, forward or backward, or even diagonally. Circle the ones you find.

Signs
Dark
Look
Fall
Trouble
Man
Shine
Earth
Cloud
Moon
Hints
Angels
Tell
Sun
Gave
Son

S	I	G	N	S	A	D	B	T
U	O	E	V	A	G	A	E	R
N	C	N	O	O	M	R	N	O
A	N	G	E	L	S	K	I	U
M	H	I	N	T	S	D	H	B
E	A	R	T	H	E	F	S	L
L	O	O	K	L	L	A	F	E
C	L	O	U	D	T	E	L	L

Getting Ready

Mark 13:32-37

Jesus told his followers to be ready for that final day when the Son of Man would come, riding on the clouds, to judge the world. On that day the sun would grow dark, the moon would no longer shine, and the stars would

HIDDEN QUESTION. There is a question hiding in the numbers and letters below. Just follow the number one until you form a word. Do the same for each of the other numbers until you discover the whole message. Then write it in the space below. Do you know the answer to the question?

2	1	4	3	5	7	2	8	3
K	W	D	T	W	W	N	C	H

4	3	8	5	8	1	9	4	7
A	E	O	H	M	H	A	Y	I

5	7	6	9	5	6	2	7	6
E	L	J	G	N	E	O	L	S

1	6	9	2	9	8	6	9	2
O	U	A	W	I	E	S	N	S

Write the question here: _____

for the End

fall from heaven! Jesus told them that no one knows when that day will be — no one except the Father. So everyone should be watching; everyone should keep eyes and ears open for that day of the Lord.

HIDDEN WORDS. These words are hiding in the letters below. Some of them are going up and down, some are going forward and backward, and some are even going diagonally. Circle the ones you find.

Jesus							
Final	J	E	S	U	S	F	E	F
Day							
Son	D	N	U	S	O	I	N	A
Man	A	A	M	A	N	N	I	T
Clouds							
World	R	E	Y	E	S	A	H	H
Sun							
Dark	K	M	O	O	N	L	S	E
Moon	C	L	O	U	D	S	A	R
Shine							
Stars	S	R	A	T	S	A	B	C
Fall	F	A	L	L	E	A	R	S
Father							
Eyes	D	L	R	O	W	D	E	F
Ears							

Costly, But

Mark 14:1—15:47

One day Jesus was visiting in the home of a man named Simon. While he was eating a meal, a woman came in with a jar of very costly perfume. She poured this perfume on Jesus' head! Some of the people in the house

HIDDEN MESSAGE. There is a message hiding in the numbers and letters below. Just follow the number one until you form a word. Do the same for each of the other numbers. Write the message in the space provided.

2	7	3	8	7	1	9	6	1	7	4
W	W	P	A	H	J	H	W	E	O	W

8	2	9	6	4	3	8	3	5	6
N	A	I	O	I	L	O	E	T	M

4	2	8	3	1	8	5	3	6	8
T	S	I	A	S	N	H	S	A	T

3	1	5	8	3	9	4	1	8	6
E	U	E	E	D	M	H	S	D	N

Write the message here: _____

Still Worth It

became very angry. They said, "Why is this woman wasting that perfume? It could have been sold and the money could have been given to the poor!" But Jesus told them to leave her alone. He said that she was getting his body ready to be buried.

HIDDEN WORDS. These words from today's story are hiding in the letters below. They might be going up or down, forward or backward, or even diagonally. Circle the ones you find.

Day
House
Simon
Angry
Home
Sold
Jesus
Money
Meal
Poor
Woman
Body
Jar
Buried
Head

D	L	O	S	Y	D	H	B
S	A	A	U	R	A	O	U
I	E	Y	S	G	E	U	R
M	M	D	E	N	H	S	I
O	O	O	J	A	R	E	E
N	H	B	P	O	O	R	D
L	A	E	M	O	N	E	Y
W	O	M	A	N	A	B	C

A Special

Mark 14:12-26

On the day before he died, Jesus ate the Passover Meal with his twelve disciples. While they were sitting at the table, Jesus told them, "One of you will betray me — one who is eating with me." This made the disciples very upset. They each began to ask him, "Surely you don't mean me, do you?" Jesus said, "It will be the one of you who dips his bread in the dish

PUZZLE TIME. You can find all of the answers to this puzzle in today's story. Try to solve it.

Across
1. The meal which Jesus shared with his disciples was the _ _ _ _ _ _ _ _ Meal.
2. The _ _ _ _ _ _ _ _ _ became very upset when Jesus said that one of them would betray him.
3. Jesus said, "Take and _ _ _, this is my body."
4. Jesus took the _ _ _ and said, "This is my blood ..."
5. Jesus said, "Whoever _ _ _ _ his bread with me is the one."
6. Judas dipped his bread in the same _ _ _ _ with Jesus.
7. _ _ _ _ _ and wine were a part of the Passover Meal.
8. Jesus _ _ _ _ the disciples some bread which he had broken.

Down
6. This special meal took place on the night before Jesus _ _ _ _.
9. On this Maundy Thursday we remember _ _ _ _ _' words and deeds.
10. This meal was the last one which the disciples _ _ _ with Jesus before he died.
11. This special feast was called the Last _ _ _ _ _ _.
12. All Jewish people eat this special _ _ _ _ at Passover time.

Supper

with me." Then Jesus took bread, gave thanks and broke it, saying, "Take and eat; this is my body." Then he took the cup, gave thanks to God, and gave it to them, saying, "This is my blood which is poured out for many ..." On this Maundy Thursday we remember Jesus' words and deeds at this Last Supper.

He Has

Mark 16:1-8

Very early the Sunday after Jesus died, Mary Magdalene, Mary the Mother of James and Salome, went to the tomb of Jesus to anoint his body with spices. They were very worried about being able to roll the stone away from the door of the tomb. But when they got there, they saw that the stone

AN EASTER PUZZLE. All of the answers to this puzzle can be found in today's story. Try to solve it.

Across
1. The angel's message was, "He has been _ _ _ _ _ _."
2. The women were too afraid to tell _ _ _ _ _ _ what had happened.
3. The women saw a young man in a white _ _ _ _.

Down
3. After they saw the angel, the women _ _ _ away.
4. Today's story happened very _ _ _ _ _ on Sunday morning.
5. The women were bringing _ _ _ _ _ _ for Jesus' body.
6. _ _ _ _ Magdalene was one of the women who met the angel.
7. The good news was that _ _ _ _ _ had been raised from the dead!
8. The women saw that the stone had been rolled away from the _ _ _ _.
9. The women had come to _ _ _ _ _ _ the body of Jesus.

Been Raised

was rolled away! They went inside and saw a young man sitting there, wearing a white robe. "Don't be afraid," he said. "I know you are looking for Jesus, who was crucified. He is not here. He has been raised!" The women ran from the tomb — very afraid — and didn't tell anyone what had happened.

www.ingramcontent.com/pod-product-compliance
Lightning Source LLC
Chambersburg PA
CBHW071758040426
42446CB00012B/2618